Why am I Angry

Jo Morgan

© 2023 Jo Morgan

All rights reserved.

No applicable part of this publication may be reproduced, stored in a retrieval system, or transmitted, in any form or by any means, electronic, mechanical, photocopying, or otherwise, without prior written permission from the copyright holder.

This Book Belongs To:

_____

_____

My mommy figured it out and cleaned me up.

I really had to pee.

I don't know why I'm angry,
I just had cookies from the store.

Mommy reaches in her bag,

she knew I wanted more

I don't know why I'm angry and I'm being grumpy too.

Oh mommy she is amazing ,
she made me fries, I really needed food.

I don't know why I'm angry,

maybe it's because it's getting dark and creepy.

Here comes mommy to tuck me in...
she is the best mom ever.

She knew that I was sleepy.

Wait looks like mommy was sleepy too!

The End!

Jo Morgan/ Author

As a proud mother and grandmother and having two children with autism, I embarked on a heartfelt journey inspired by my children's autism diagnoses. Recognizing the misconceptions people have about this condition, I felt compelled to create books that offer solace to parents navigating the unique challenges, highs, and lows of raising children on the spectrum. My aim is not only to reassure parents that they're not alone but also to let these incredible kids know that their experiences are understood, cherished, and celebrated through my books, I hope to spread awareness, empathy, and the understanding that while a child with autism may have their own set of highs, lows, and everything in between, they are undeniably special and extraordinary in their own right.

www.YoursTrulyJoMorgan.com

Why Am I Angry is the story of the daily life of a nonverbal little boy with autism, his mother, and their mission to communicate and work together to fulfill his needs and wants. Jo Morgan crafts her story with authentic, firsthand experience from her life as a single mom of an autistic child, making it an educational experience for parents seeking understanding, guidance, and patience. The fun, brightly colored pictures and engaging text will keep little readers fascinated while forming a connection for children and parents alike, assuring them they are not alone.

www.ingramcontent.com/pod-product-compliance
Lightning Source LLC
LaVergne TN
LVHW070433070526
838199LV00014B/499